START-UP HISTORY

Seaside holidays

Stewart Ross

W

FRANKLIN WATTS
LONDON • SYDNEY

First published in 2014 by Franklin Watts

Copyright © White-Thomson Publishing 2014

Franklin Watts
338 Euston Road
London NW1 3BH

Franklin Watts Australia
Level 17/207 Kent Street
Sydney, NSW 2000

Produced for Franklin Watts by
White-Thomson Publishing Ltd

www.wtpub.co.uk
+44 (0) 843 208 7460

Editor: Anna Lee
Consultant: Norah Granger
Designer: Tessa Barwick

This book was first published by Evans Brothers Ltd.
It has been revised and fully updated in line with the KS1
history curriculum.

A CIP catalogue record for this book is available from the
British Library.

Dewey no: 394.2'69146
Hardback ISBN: 9781 4451 3496 3
Library eBook ISBN: 978 1 4451 3497 0

Printed in China

Franklin Watts is a division of Hachette Children's Books,
an Hachette UK company.
www.hachette.co.uk

Picture Acknowledgements: Corbis: 8b, 15t, 20, cover
main; Dreamstime: 6, 7, 8t, 18; Getty: 4, 5t; Impact: 21;
Mary Evans: 5b, 10-11dps, 10b, 15b, 19l, 19r; Science and
Society Picture Library: 9; Shutterstock: 14, cover t, cover
b; Topfoto: 12-13dps, 16-17dps, 19 (Topham/Chapman),
20 (Topham Picturepoint). The picture on page 5t is
reproduced courtesy of the Royal British Legion.

Every effort has been made to clear copyright. Should there
be any inadvertent omission, please apply to the publisher
for rectification.

Every effort has been made by the Publishers to ensure that
the websites featured in this book are suitable for children,
that they are of the highest educational value and that they
contain no inappropriate or offensive material. However,
because of the nature of the Internet, it is impossible to
guarantee that the contents of these sites will not be altered.
We strongly advise that Internet access is supervised by a
responsible adult.

Contents

Seaside holidays now and in the past

These people are on holiday.
They are at the seaside.

holiday   seaside   years

▶ **This family is on holiday 50 years ago.**

▼ **Here are people at the seaside almost 100 years ago.**

How are their clothes different from today's clothes?

ago   clothes   different   today

January	February	March	April	May	June

winter ....➤ spring

This is a **timeline** of a year.
These are the **months** of the year.
These are the **seasons**........

We have **summer** holidays in July and August.

What other holidays can you think of?

winter spring timeline months

have holidays?

July	August	September	October	November	December

summer   autumn   winter

Some people like to visit the **beach** **in** **winter**.

seasons summer autumn beach

How shall we get there?

▶ **These people are arriving for a seaside holiday.**

They have gone abroad by plane.

◀ **This family has gone to the seaside by car.**

They will stay in their caravan.

abroad   plane   car

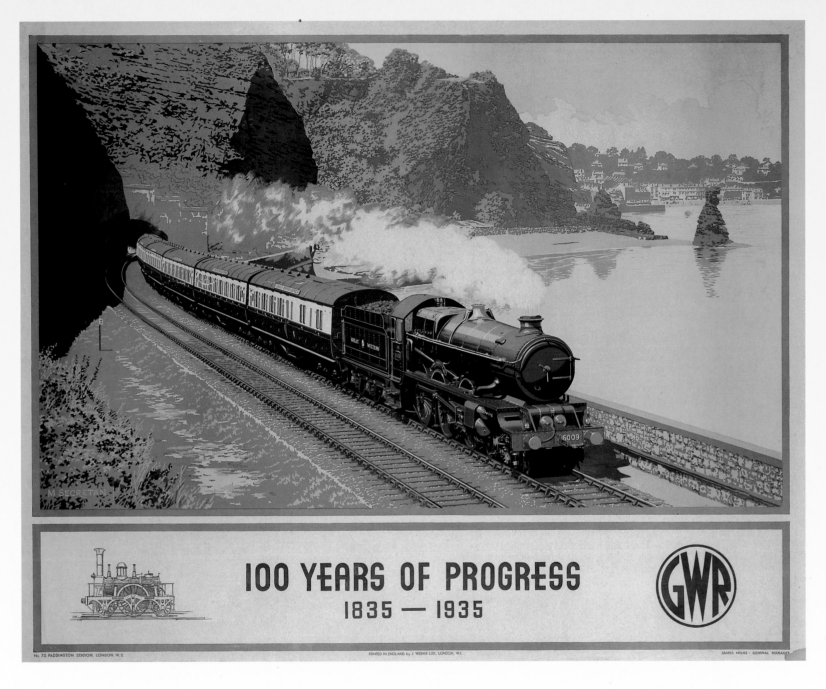

Long ago, steam engines pulled trains.
The train in this poster is taking people to the seaside.

caravan   steam engines   poster   9
....

Hooray! We've arrived!

In the past,
people went to the seaside
in buses called charabancs.

How are these charabancs
different from buses today?

past   buses

Can you think
of some other ways
of going to the seaside?

charabancs

Looking at the past

What a crowded beach!
Is this a modern photograph?
Or was it taken long ago?

You can find out if you look at:

the pram

the food stalls

the men's hats

the women's dresses

modern   photograph

This is a
photograph
of Herne Bay
in Kent.
It was taken
almost 70
years ago.

long ago   food stalls

Swimsuits now and then

These pictures are from different times in the past.

The most recent photograph was taken
about 5 years ago.

recent

▶ **This photograph was taken about 70 years ago.**

◀ **The oldest photograph was taken about 80 years ago.**

How are the swimsuits on these pages different?

oldest   swimsuits   15

Fun at the seaside!

This photograph was taken about 100 years ago.

The people are listening to the band in the bandstand.

Find these things in the picture: houses, clothes, pier, parasols, bicycles.

Which are the same as nowadays?

Which are different?

band   bandstand   pier

parasols   **nowadays**

More fun at the seaside!

Here is a modern seaside ride.

ride

▶ Here is a photograph of a wooden rollercoaster ride from 60 years ago.

▲ This photograph of a family playing on the beach was taken about 90 years ago.

What game are they playing?

rollercoaster

19

Punch and Judy

Here are two photographs of children watching Punch and Judy shows.

One was taken recently. One was taken in the past.

at the beach

What are the differences between them?

How are they the same?

same

Further information for

New history and seaside holiday words listed in the text:

abroad	caravan	months	poster	spring
ago	charabancs	nowadays	Punch and Judy	steam engine
autumn	clothes	oldest	recent	summer
band	different	parasols	ride	swimsuits
bandstand	food stalls	past	rollercoaster	timeline
beach	holiday	photograph	same	today
buses	long ago	pier	seaside	winter
car	modern	plane	seasons	years

Background Information

A BRIEF CHRONOLOGY

MIDDLE AGES People not expected to work on 'holy days'.

LATE 17th CENTURY ONWARDS 'Grand Tour' of Europe fashionable with the wealthy.
Rising popularity of spas such as Bath and Buxton.

18th CENTURY Seaside resorts become fashionable and popular with the wealthy, e.g. Scarborough, Weymouth and Ramsgate.
Bathing machines appear.

EARLY 19th CENTURY First 'tourist' (word first used in 1800) hotels built in romantic beauty spots, e.g. Lake District.
Middle classes visit the seaside.
1840s: First seaside excursion trains herald the arrival of working class holidaymakers.
The wealthy flee to more exclusive resorts or abroad.

MID-19th CENTURY Rise of Blackpool as a working-class resort.
Continental tourism flourishing.
Although only four official public holidays, many northern businesses close for their local Wakes or Feast (traditional festivals).

LATE 19th CENTURY

1871 The government introduces four more public holidays.
Significant numbers of the working class taking seaside holidays of several nights away from home, assisted by employers' schemes, Sunday schools and friendly societies.

FIRST HALF OF 20th CENTURY Heyday of the British seaside holiday.
1937 3 million workers have some paid holiday.
First holiday camp (Butlins) opens.
Leisure 'industry' emerging.

Parents and Teachers

1938 Holidays with Pay Act: 14 million workers now have some paid holiday.

1950-2015

1951 25 million people taking holidays in Britain.

1960s Emergence of the mass 'package tour' business.

1971 34 million people taking holidays in Britain. Thereafter the figure declines. 7 million holidaying abroad.

1984 16 million holidaying abroad.
Some once-famous seaside resorts in decline.
Others (e.g. Brighton) remain buoyant.

Possible Activities:

Invite an adult to come and talk about their experiences of seaside holidays in the past.

Produce a map of Britain's seaside resorts.

Make a class frieze timeline for the current year and mark all holidays, religious and otherwise, on it.

Make a collection of seaside holiday objects: postcards, buckets and spades, photographs, seaweed, etc.

Some Topics for Discussion:

How have seaside holidays changed from (a) parents' time (b) grandparents' time?

What are the advantages/disadvantages of seaside holidays abroad?

How might holidaymakers be bad for the seaside? (Pollution, environmental damage, etc.)

Further Information

BOOKS

FOR CHILDREN

History Snapshots: The Seaside by Sarah Ridley (Franklin Watts, 2011)

Popcorn: Seaside Holidays by Dereen Taylor (Wayland, 2010)

The Story of: Seaside Holidays by Anita Ganeri (Raintree, 2008)

Ways into History: Seaside Holidays by Sally Hewitt (Watts, 2012)

Your Local Area: Seaside by Ruth Thomson (Wayland, 2012)

FOR ADULTS

The British Seaside Holiday by Kathryn Ferry (Shire History, 2009)

Designing the Seaside by Fred Gray (Reaktion Books, 2009)

WEBSITES

http://www.tes.co.uk/teaching-resource/Seaside-holidays-then-and-now-3005853/

http://www.heritage-explorer.co.uk/web/he/teachingactivitiesdetail.aspx?id=11006&crit=&ctid=48

http://www.westsussex.gov.uk/learning/learning_resources/west_sussex_seaside_holidays_i/learn_about_seaside_holidays_i.aspx

PLACES TO VISIT

Several seaside resorts have fascinating local history museums, for example the Margate Museum, Kent.

Index